RESCUE RIDERS

AMBULANCES
TO THE RESCUE!

AMBULANCE

BY FRANCES NAGLE

Gareth Stevens
PUBLISHING

Please visit our website, www.garethstevens.com. For a free color catalog of all our high-quality books, call toll free 1-800-542-2595 or fax 1-877-542-2596.

Library of Congress Cataloging-in-Publication Data
Names: Nagle, Frances, 1959- author.
Title: Ambulances to the rescue! / Frances Nagle.
Description: New York : Gareth Stevens Publishing, [2023] | Series: Rescue riders | Includes bibliographical references and index.
Identifiers: LCCN 2021046639 (print) | LCCN 2021046640 (ebook) | ISBN 9781538278444 (set) | ISBN 9781538278451 (library binding) | ISBN 9781538278437 (paperback) | ISBN 9781538278468 (ebook)
Subjects: LCSH: Ambulance service–Juvenile literature. | Emergency medicine–Juvenile literature. | Ambulances–Juvenile literature.
Classification: LCC RA995 .N34 2023 (print) | LCC RA995 (ebook) | DDC 362.18/8–dc23/eng/20211025
LC record available at https://lccn.loc.gov/2021046639
LC ebook record available at https://lccn.loc.gov/2021046640

Published in 2023 by
Gareth Stevens Publishing
29 E. 21st Street
New York, NY 10010

Portions of this work were originally authored by B. J. Best and published as *Ambulances*. All new material this edition authored by Frances Nagle.

Designer: Leslie Taylor
Editor: Kristen Nelson

Photo credits: Cover OgnjenO/Shutterstock.com; pp. 2-24 (background texture) Pixel Embargo/Shutterstock.com; p. 5 temp-64GTX/Shutterstock.com; p. 7 pbk-pg/Shutterstock.com; p. 9 Hypervision Creative/Shutterstock.com; p. 11 michaeljung/Shutterstock.com; pp. 13, 17 Iakov Filimonov/Shutterstock.com; p. 15 Motortion Films/Shutterstock.com; p. 19 Gervasio S. _ Eureka_89/Shutterstock.com; p. 21 Tyler Olson/Shutterstock.com.

Printed in the United States of America

CPSIA compliance information: Batch #CSGS23: For further information contact Gareth Stevens, New York, New York at 1-800-542-2595.

Find us on

CONTENTS

Boldface words appear in the glossary.

Emergency!

Do you hear a **siren**? It might be an ambulance on the way to help someone! An ambulance is an emergency vehicle. Emergency vehicles are cars, trucks, and vans that are used to respond to unexpected or dangerous **situations**.

5

Ambulances are emergency vehicles that go to help people who are sick or hurt. Sometimes people call for an ambulance to come. Sometimes they arrive at an emergency with other emergency vehicles like fire trucks or police cars.

Kinds of Ambulances

Some big cities have hundreds of ambulances! Hospitals and fire departments have them. There are also special companies that **operate** ambulances. Ambulances are often trucks or **cargo** vans. A helicopter or small airplane can be an ambulance too!

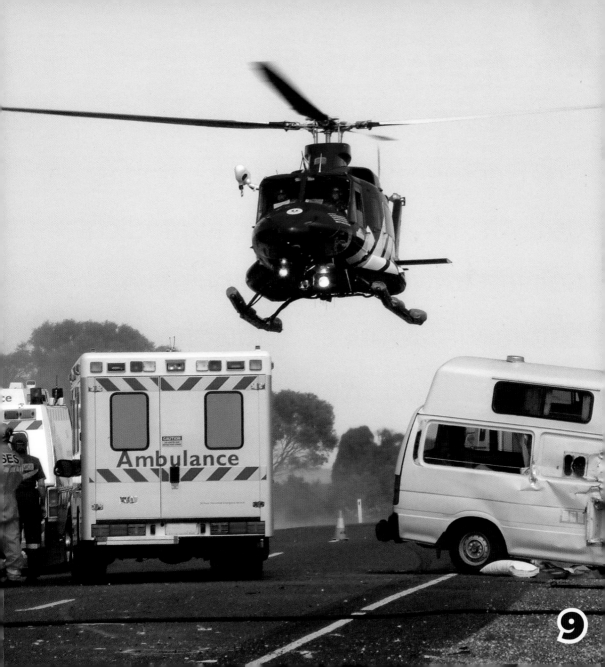

9

Emergency Workers

People who work in ambulances are Emergency **Medical** Technicians, or EMTs. EMTs have special medical training to work in an ambulance. Paramedics work in ambulances too. They have even more medical training than EMTs. EMTs and paramedics both know how to handle emergencies!

Getting the Call

Ambulances respond to many kinds of emergencies. They go to fires. They are called for car crashes. If someone has a bad fall or other **injury**, ambulances are often called. EMTs and paramedics are ready for any of these situations.

13

When EMTs get an emergency call, they move quickly! They can be on the road in the ambulance in minutes. They often turn on the siren and flashing lights. This tells others on the road to move out of the way. They drive fast!

15

The Ambulance Ride

EMTs and paramedics can help someone who is sick or hurt right away. But, many times, their main job is to get a person to a hospital. The **patient** rides in the back of the ambulance.

The ambulance has many medical tools in the back. They have special cots with wheels for moving patients. They have bandages and **medicines**. They have tools to help people breathe. They even have flashlights and blankets. Ambulances are ready for any situation they encounter!

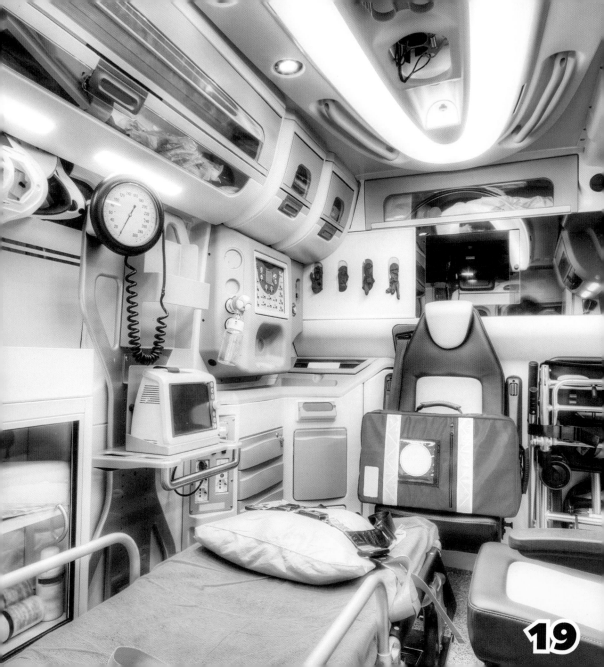

At the Hospital

Ambulances drive patients to a hospital. There, doctors and nurses will take care of the patient. The EMTs and paramedics may then get another emergency call. They drive away to help. Ambulances help save lives!

GLOSSARY

cargo: goods carried by plane, train, or other vehicle

injury: harm or damage

medical: having to do with care given by doctors or other health care workers

medicine: a drug taken to make a sick person well

operate: to have control of something

patient: a person who gets medical care

siren: a piece of equipment that makes a loud, high-pitched warning sound

situation: the conditions and events happening at a certain time and place

FOR MORE INFORMATION

BOOKS

Harris, Bizzy. *Ambulances*. Minneapolis, MN: Jump! Inc., 2022.

Rossiter, Brienna. *Big Machines for Fire and Rescue*. Lake Elmo, MN: Focus Readers, 2021.

WEBSITES

Ambulance
kids.kiddle.co/Ambulance

Get more information about what's inside an ambulance and how they help people here.

Rescue Vehicle Coloring Pages
supercoloring.com/coloring-pages/transport/rescue-vehicles

Ask an adult to help you download and print some coloring pages of emergency vehicles.

INDEX